How to Teach Your Craft
Creating Revenue by Teaching Classes and Workshops

by Amanda Gail

amanda@teachcraftclasses.com

www.teachcraftclasses.com

Printed in the United States of America
First Printing, 2015
ISBN 978-0-9861316-0-8

Ordering Information:
Wholesale sales. Special discounts are available on quantity purchases. For details, contact the publisher at the email address above.

Cover Images:
© geocislariu/Dollar Photo Club
© olya_dn/Dollar Photo Club
© Ionescu Bogdan/Dollar Photo Club
© karenkh/Dollar Photo Club
© Africa Studio/Dollar Photo Club
© Africa Studio/Dollar Photo Club
© trionis/Dollar Photo Club
© Yeko Photo Studio/Dollar Photo Club

Dedication

This book is dedicated to my fellow crafters who wish to awaken joy in others by teaching their craft.

Amanda Gail

Table of Contents

Acknowledgements

It has been my aim to write a book for quite a long time. I've written all sorts of digital publications such as eBooks and eZines, but there was always something so unattainable about actually writing and having a book printed. With the help of a wonderful tribe of people surrounding me and encouraging me, I did it!

So *How to Teach Your Craft: Creating Revenue by Teaching Classes and Workshops*, my first printed book has been completed with support and inspiration from:

Holly Port, my best friend, my co-teacher and author of *Make it Fizz: A Guide to Making Bathtub Treats*. Holly constantly gave me encouragement and held me accountable, asking how many pages I'd written or what I'd done to keep the book going. She was one of my biggest cheerleaders during this process, especially early on. Thank you, Holly!

Benjamin Aaron, my partner in life, co-director of Lovin' Soap Project and owner of Maker's Climb. Benjamin provided encouragement and guidance throughout the process, editing help, content help, comic relief and grounding. Thanks, Benjamin!

Sheila Aaron, Benjamin's Mama, who carefully and meticulously edited the book. I never knew I used so many unnecessary words. Thank you, Mama Shelia!

And a whole tribe of people who read early drafts and gave me wonderful feedback such as Rachel Turner, Renee Lillie, Sindy Anderson, Sue Finley and my sister, Megan Smith.

"It is the supreme art of the teacher to awaken joy in creative expression and knowledge."

-Albert Einstein

Amanda Gail

Introduction

Hello. My name is Amanda Gail and I am a craft junky.

I have been through obsessive crafty fits of knitting, jewelry making, painting, paper crafting and just about any other craft you could think of. On one feverishly creative day, I went to feed my serial crafting addiction by visiting the local craft supply store. Walking down the aisles of scrapbooking paper, paint and jewelry making supplies, nothing was speaking to me. I desired something different, something that I hadn't done before. I came upon the soap and candle aisle and my holy grail was discovered. Soap. I hastily bought soap base, color, scent, molds and cute little boxes for packaging and headed home to jump head first into the craft. I soon became obsessed with soapmaking and was making it just about every weekend.

I so fell in love with soapmaking that I started a business selling soap and body products. I sold my delicious smelling bath treats at the local farmer's market and at craft shows almost every weekend. I had an Etsy shop and even my own website. Nevertheless, I quickly discovered that my desire was not selling product; it was teaching.

Putting ideas to action, I began teaching people how to make soap, formulate recipes and troubleshoot potential snags in the soapmaking process at two different local Dallas soap and bodycare suppliers. With the onset and pressures of online competition, both local suppliers (which happened to be my classrooms) closed their doors, so I was forced to make a decision – say "oh well, it wasn't meant to be," or go out on my own and start teaching independently. I chose the latter. I arranged classes and bootcamps in the Dallas-Fort Worth area and Austin, Texas. Soon thereafter, I began teaching in New York as a guest teacher, which eventually led me to teaching my craft—my passion—internationally in the developing nations of Haiti and Uganda.

So why am I writing this book?

Because I've been there, messed up, had some not-so-great classes and learned many lessons along the way. I've met so many people, some experts in their field of craft, who would love to teach, but don't have the know-how to make it happen or simply don't know where to start. This book is for the crafter who is ready and willing to take the leap into instructing, guiding and ultimately, leading.

I once taught a demonstration-only class hosted by a craft store. They charged quite a bit for it and students watched while I went through the process. The craft storeowner assumed having students make their own soap would be too dangerous. Boring. Students revolted and threw vegetables. Okay, not really, but I'm sure if there were baskets of rotten tomatoes sitting by the door they would have chucked a few my way as they disappointedly walked out.

Students want to get their hands dirty, especially creative, crafty and artistic makers who live to use their hands to create.

I once taught a soapmaking class where the difficulty level of the technique used was not matched to the students' skill level. There were tears of frustration and disappointment. If one of my students leaves a class not having the confidence to repeat the process I've taught, I have failed them.

My mission as a teacher is to have each student walk away knowing they can go home and repeat the process that I have taught them.

I once partnered with a friend to do a multi-class workshop without any kind of contract or agreed upon compensation plan. The situation quickly got bad. We thought that because we were friends, we would be good co-teachers and everything would just magically work out. We never got on the same page. Now we're not even friends.

I will never enter into a collaborative teaching situation without firmly agreeing upon policies, procedures, financial decisions and marketing obligations.

There have been many failures and lessons learned during my journey into and through teaching classes and workshops around the United States and abroad. The above examples are only a few lessons learned; more will be shared throughout this book.

I've grown my for-profit teaching business into my main income generator, all the while cultivating a 501(c)(3) not-for-profit organization with my partner, developed around teaching my craft, which I'll share more about later.

I'm going to help you build your teaching empire and save you some headache and maybe even some heartache along the way.

Who Should Read This Book?

This book is for the crafter or artist who has a craving or even just a curious interest in teaching their craft. Perhaps you already sell your crafted items but are looking for additional revenue streams. Or perhaps, like me, you are looking for another way to earn income through your craft or trade without having to sell what you create.

This book is also for the craft storeowner or studio owner who is interested in providing classes to boost revenue and draw in more customers.

I wrote this book because I am often asked questions about teaching classes and workshops from fellow crafters, such as:

- How do you decide what to teach?

- Do you provide a handout?

- How do you find students and fill up classes?

- How do you take registrations?

- How do you find guest teachers?

- Do you teach hands-on classes?

- Do you have insurance?

- How do you find a place to teach?

This book will answer many of these questions and then some. I don't consider myself an absolute expert on the topic, but I do have years of experience from which others can learn. Students travel from all over, even from out of the country, to participate in multiple day workshops that I put together. I've taught everything from single classes to multiple day workshops to private lessons. I've taught for myself, for others and with others. I am writing this book from the perspective of teaching classes in my industry—handcrafted soap and body products—so your industry might vary on many things, including class format, pricing, etc., so keep that in mind as you read.

This book will provide you with the basic process for coming up with your own classes and provide tips-and-tricks along the way to help you build your teaching empire.

Amanda Gail

Chapter 1: Becoming a Teacher

My story.

When I began making soap in Texas, I was fortunate to have a few local soap suppliers in town. Instead of merely ordering supplies online, I could go buy supplies on the weekends and hang out with the shop owners and fellow customers, talking soap and body product formulations. If anybody who walked into the store needed advice or directions for making a certain soap or product, I eagerly made myself available to help. One of the shop owners would even point customers my way if they had questions that needed answers! I loved it. I spent a considerable amount of time at the supplier's shops on the weekends, in addition to constantly emailing and talking to people who needed help getting started in the trade.

The need for local classes was glaringly obvious where I lived and it might be where you live as well.

I asked one of the shop owners if he would be interested in having me teach classes. What's the worst he could say? I presented him with a plan that included pricing, class content, materials needed, etc. I explained how it would be beneficial for both of us, as classes would draw in students who would then turn into customers buying the supplies they needed to craft what they had just learned from me. Without even reading my plan, he eagerly agreed. We decided on a 50/50 split and we were off. I will always remember my first class and my first student, Minnie Daniel.

I had many fun classes teaching for that supplier, including a class of firefighters who made candles during downtime at the fire station. They wanted to add soapmaking to their repertoire, so they took a class. My students ranged from homemakers to lawyers, teachers to medical workers. I met so many wonderful people teaching there.

But alas, that supplier eventually went out of business, so I simply moved my classes to another supplier in town. I taught for them for about six months with a similar arrangement. Unfortunately, they eventually shut their business down as well, with the onset of more and more online supplier competition within the industry.

With no more suppliers in town to partner with, I was now on my own. This was when my teaching career really took off. Teaching for the suppliers was great, but I was limited to what *they* would allow, the price *they* wanted to charge, *their* schedule and the format that *they* approved. I now had complete control of my soapmaking classes and the freedom to creatively develop my very own content and format, and it was exciting! I set up a website that took registrations and added a variety of classes to my lineup. I expanded into a new city and added bootcamp-style workshops to my offerings. Students could then take three to five classes over the course of a weekend. I brought in guest teachers who helped bring in new and fresh classes and before long, I was literally traveling the world to teach soapmaking.

Why Teach?

Supplementary Income

Teaching can provide an additional revenue stream to add to your regular business operations. Perhaps you're a crafter and you have an Etsy shop, your own website or a brick-and-mortar storefront where you sell your wares to earn an income. Or maybe you sell supplies to crafters. You might be doing okay, but you could use a bit of additional income to purchase supplies, cover rent or just give yourself some breathing room.

The handcrafted marketplace is booming, which lends to a vast increase in curiosity and demand from people who want to learn the limitless varieties of crafts. There is a movement towards doing things with our own hands. People are starting to sew again, to knit, to make their own natural body care products. People are even crafting their own liqueurs and brewing their own beer. The craft market is growing everyday, therefore the demand for classes is growing right along with it. Simply teaching one class a month can provide from $50 to $1000 in income, depending on your industry and the prices you charge.

Alternative to Selling Product

Teaching can provide you an income without having to produce product to sell. Perhaps you're an ardent crafter. You love to make ceramics. But turning your love of ceramics into a business requires keeping up with production, even when you're not feeling crafty. Sometimes when we turn what we love into a business it kills the passion. Teaching still allows you to create revenue doing what you love but in a way that works best for artists and crafters that don't want to sell their art or crafts.

This is what happened to me. I reached burnout selling my soap and just didn't like that part of the craft; however, I wanted to earn a living doing what I love. Now I teach, and it brings great delight to me to be able to introduce others to the craft.

Occasionally, the potential income stream from teaching your craft is far more lucrative than selling the items made from your craft.

Gain Notoriety as an Industry Expert

Teaching classes sets you up as an industry expert, making you stand out in your craft. Individuals and organizations will come to you as you prove yourself to be a reliable resource for information and industry advice. Media sources, whether online, print or television, will seek you out for your expertise by means of interviews and other media coverage.

You will gain more exposure for yourself and your business by becoming an industry educator and expert, which could boost your overall sales if you do sell what you make.

As a Way to Travel and See the World

Teaching classes has led me to cities, states and even countries that I would have never dreamed of visiting. I've taught in New York, Texas, Florida, Missouri, North Carolina, Tennessee, Alabama and even Haiti and Uganda. I started a not-for-profit, The Lovin' Soap Project, in which my partner and I teach soapmaking to women in developing countries and help them start businesses. You can elect to teach local classes only or you can open yourself up to teaching classes anywhere your heart desires. There is no limit!

You never know the heights teaching will take you and whom you will meet along the way. Let's get started!

Are You a Teacher?

Not everyone is a teacher. Being an effective teacher takes personality to hold your students' attention, commitment to always learn more of your craft, and especially openness. That means if you are willing to share, you must share all. There are people in my industry who are afraid of sharing *this* technique or *that* trade secret, as I'm sure there are those in your industry as well. Some feel that their students will steal customers or steal their part of the market or even fear that their students will become better than the teacher. *These people should not teach.*

Some people have the initial mindset that if they are teaching, they are creating competition. Sure, you're creating other crafters who will be doing something similar to you, but they aren't you. And if someone wants to learn your craft, they're going to. *Why not be the one who earns the income from it?*

Be a teacher who is open, honest and dedicated to your students, and you'll be rewarded with more class signups from previous students and from word-of-mouth referrals.

What are Your Options?

There are many different ways to deliver your content. You can provide single classes, online webinars, hands-on workshops or weekend long bootcamps. You can teach classes weekly or you can hold workshops once a month. Teaching offers flexibility, so that you can work around any schedule you currently have.

Classes, workshops, intensives, bootcamps, seminars, webinars...there are various definitions for these terms, but typically they are defined as follows:

Classes

A class is a course of instruction that can be a couple of hours on a single day or can be a series of days that expands weeks or even months. If you teach a painting class for example, it can be a Wednesday night from 6-9 p.m., or it can be a series of four Wednesday nights from 6-9 p.m.

Workshops

A workshop is an event that emphasizes the sharing of ideas, instruction, a demonstration or real world application of techniques or learned skills. Workshops can be a couple of hours in a single day or can be multiple days, keeping in mind that they emphasize *hands-on* instruction.

Bootcamps & Intensives

Bootcamps and intensives are a series of classes spread out over a weekend or even a week. They are usually more rigorous and intensive in training, hence the term bootcamp taken from military jargon. Typically, a large amount of information is presented in a short amount of time. Bootcamps are great for drawing in out-of-town students who can sign up for one weekend and knock out several of your classes at one time.

I love producing soapmaking bootcamps and will plan five classes over three days. For example, a typical soapmaking weekend schedule is:

Soapmaking Bootcamp Weekend Schedule

Friday (6 p.m. – 9 p.m.) – Basic Soapmaking
Saturday (9 a.m. – noon) – Advanced Soapmaking: Coloring Techniques
Saturday (noon – 1 p.m.) – Lunch
Saturday (1 p.m. – 4 p.m.) – Advanced Soapmaking: Goat Milk Soap
Sunday (9 a.m. – noon) – Advanced Soapmaking: Beer and Wine Soap
Sunday (noon - 1 p.m.) – Lunch
Sunday (1 p.m. – 4 p.m.) – Advanced Soapmaking: Liquid Soapmaking

Private Classes

Private classes are classes in which a student signs up to get one-on-one instruction from you. He or she is the only one in class. You can usually charge more for these types of classes because you are losing out on income by just having one student in the class. You can even find students who will pay your travel expenses to come to them. Charge more for these classes, as one-on-one instruction should come at a premium.

You can also offer private classes for group events, birthday parties, showers, ladies nights and corporate events.

Online Classes and Webinars

You can greatly expand the reach of your instructional content by creating online classrooms. Webinars are seminars delivered online to a live audience in which students can participate by asking questions or taking part in discussions.

It is a great way to gain students from all over the world! And since expenses are minimal, you can charge less for the classes and even pocket more of the profit.

Kid's Classes

Kid's classes are a great market to tap into. Parents are forever looking for after school and summer activities for their kids. If your craft or art is something kids can do, consider teaching kid's classes as well as adult. You can even expand that into offering packages for birthdays, scouting groups, youth groups, school groups and more.

Chapter 2: For Whom Will You be Teaching?

I started my teaching career teaching for two local suppliers. I taught a basic soapmaking class which didn't really focus on artistic implementation or fancier techniques, like swirling colors. I remember asking the supplier if I could branch out and offer some advanced classes that would instruct students on coloring techniques and swirling soap designs. They had no interest; they just wanted me to teach a basic class. I was also only allowed to schedule classes on two Saturday mornings a month. Because they were closed at 6 pm, I couldn't teach Friday or Saturday evenings.

After I started creating my own classes and workshops, I had complete control over every aspect. I chose the days I wanted to teach, adding Friday night classes and full weekend bootcamps to the schedule instead of just Saturdays. I added advanced techniques and designs to my class offerings, which covered topics such as liquid soapmaking, color swirling and more.

I've had experience teaching for someone else and teaching for myself. Let's talk about both.

Teaching for Someone Else

Teaching for someone else is a great way to break into a career as a craft instructor. If you aren't ready to do it alone, this is a great path for you. Following are some places that are seeking teachers.

- A craft shop or supplier: Contact a major chain such as Michael's or find a local supplier that sells something related to your craft such as yarn, scrapbooking supplies, soapmaking supplies or sewing machines.

- A college or university: Contact your local university or community college. In addition to credit classes, most colleges offer continuing education or community education type classes for adults.

- A community center: Most cities have community centers that offer community classes ranging from fitness and sports to lifestyle and crafts.

- An art or craft studio: Craft studios are popping up all over in which students come in and create their own ceramics or paint their own picture (while often enjoying a glass of wine). Do an Internet search for local craft studios and see what you can find.

Making Contact and Submitting a Class Proposal

First, make contact with the business. This can be done in person, by email or by calling the business.

- Make contact in person: Take a class project to the business. We'll talk more about class projects in chapter 3. Ask for the person in charge of classes and introduce yourself. Take your sample and show them what you'd like to teach. Make sure your technique or design is unique. They are going to look at your class project sample and ask themselves, will my students and/or customers want to make this?

- Make contact by email: Send an email and include a picture of the class project, a short bio and a brief statement that you are interested in teaching classes at their place and that you'd love to talk to them about it.

- Make contact by phone: Contact by phone seems to be the least effective. If you do decide to call a business or organization, make sure to get the right person on the phone. Ask for the individual that coordinates classes and introduce yourself. This will usually need to be followed up with an email containing more information or a visit in person.

After making initial contact, the business will probably ask for a proposal for the class. Your proposal should include:

- Your bio and experience: Have you taught classes before? Do you own a business selling what you make? What is your past experience in the industry and why are you qualified to teach classes? We'll talk more about writing a bio in chapter 10.

- The class description: A description of what the students will learn and what they will experience in class. We'll talk more about class descriptions in chapter 6.

- A picture of the class project: They will want to see what you will be making in class as a class project.

- A list of supplies and equipment needed: What materials will each student need to complete his or her project? What equipment is required per student? If you are teaching knitting classes, perhaps each student will receive a pair of needles and some yarn. Or perhaps you will require that the students bring needles and yarn to class.

I usually start off by sending the information above; once they've expressed interest in the class, class fees and teacher fees will be discussed. They might have a standard fee in place or they might be flexible. Don't be afraid to negotiate.

How Much do You Get Paid?

It varies, depending on whom you teach for. Usually when you teach for someone else, you will be paid a set hourly wage as an employee or you will be paid a set fee per class or a set percentage per class if you are a contractor.

When teaching for someone else, most of the logistics are taken care of by the host; you are just there to teach. Sometimes the host will do all of the marketing and promotion or sometimes you might be required to help with that. If you are getting a percentage per class, it will certainly be in your best interest to help get signups.

Pros of Teaching for Someone Else

- You don't have to worry about renting a space.

- You don't have to worry about signup software, receiving payments, credit card processing or dealing with student registrations.

- You don't usually have to worry about purchasing supplies and equipment; however, some places require the teacher bring supplies and collect a supply fee from the students.

Cons of Teaching for Someone Else

- You are limited in many ways including class content, class format, class schedules and class pricing.

- You have to share the profit.

Teaching for Yourself

Teaching for yourself and coming up with your own classes and workshops is going to give you the most flexibility and potential for creating revenue. However, it is also going to take the most work and effort.

This book mainly focuses on creating your own classes and workshops; however, some of the techniques and ideas are great for those wanting to teach for a host and can be used to create proposal content.

Chapter 3: What will you Teach?

Coming Up with Class Ideas

The secret to having a successful and profitable teaching business is to offer an array of classes that offers your students more and more choices.

I teach soapmaking classes. When I started teaching, I taught only one class that combined the basics of soapmaking with advanced topics such as coloring techniques and design. Since it was the only class I taught, there were no further class offerings for the students to take.

I soon wised up and broke that class into two classes, a basic class and an advanced color and design class. The basic class was required before enrolling in the advanced class. Students would often sign up for both!

Now I've added even more classes. I offer Basic Soapmaking, Advanced Color and Swirling, Cupcakes and Piping Techniques, Beer and Wine Soapmaking, Making Soap with Milk, Liquid Soapmaking, Mold Making and more. I've had several students start with the basic soapmaking class, and then once they were hooked, would sign up for the advanced classes.

Make a List of Possible Class Ideas for your Craft

Start with the basics of your craft. Strip it down. What is the most basic process when it comes to doing what you do? Once you determine that, add advanced techniques, patterns and designs.

I stick to one beginner class and offer multiple advanced classes. Another option would be to offer several *levels* of classes including Beginner, Basic, Intermediate, Advanced and Expert. For example:

Beginner Soapmaking
Advanced Soapmaking: Layering Soap
Advanced Soapmaking: Swirling
Advanced Soapmaking: Liquid Soap

OR

Beginner Soapmaking
Basic Soapmaking: Layering Soap
Intermediate Soapmaking: Swirling
Advanced Soapmaking: Liquid Soap

Be sure to take a look at popular cultural trends when designing your classes. People get obsessive over popular cultural trends (i.e. cupcakes and vampires) and will pay money to do anything that involves the trend. Someone who isn't even interested in sewing might sign up to sew that adorable little cupcake pincushion. Other classes that come to mind following the cupcake trend in different industries including soap cupcakes, making cupcake beads, baking cupcakes, painting cupcakes, knitting cupcakes, etc. Take a close look at popular cultural trends and see if you can benefit from the crazes as you design your classes. As trends change often, so will these special classes. You might only teach the cupcake themed class for six months and move on to something else. Here are some examples from different industries:

Sewing
Beginner Sewing
Advanced Sewing: Modern Blouse
Advanced Sewing: Zipper Techniques
Advanced Sewing: Adorable Cupcake Pincushion

Paper-Crafting
Beginner Paper-crafting
Basic Paper-crafting: Handmade Holiday Card
Intermediate Paper-crafting: Summer Fun Scrapbook Page
Advanced Paper-crafting: Chic Paper Photo Frame

Fused Glass
Beginner Fused Glass
Advanced Fused Glass: Multi Colored Pendent
Advanced Fused Glass: Wine Stopper
Advanced Fused Glass: Glass Flower Tiles
Open Studio

You get the point! Any trade or craft has a basic process, and moves on to advanced variations or techniques from which a variety of classes can then be developed.

Open Studio or Open Lab Times

Another way to draw in students and create a bit of additional income is to offer open lab or studio times. A student (who already has experience in the craft) rents a time slot to come in and use your materials and/or equipment to craft. This works great for industries in which expensive equipment is required, such as a kiln for pottery or glass blowing, or welding equipment for art welding. You could charge an equipment usage fee or you could charge based on materials being used (clay, paint, etc.).

Begin by writing out 5-10 ideas for classes. Now don't try to do them all at once...especially if you are new to teaching. Pick about three or four and start with those, adding the others when you feel comfortable and when students demand it!

Here is my list for soapmaking classes.

Soapmaking

Basic Soapmaking
Advanced Soapmaking: Coloring Techniques
Advanced Soapmaking: Soaping with Goat Milk
Advanced Soapmaking: Soaping with Beer and Wine
Advanced Soapmaking: Liquid Soapmaking
Advanced Soapmaking: Piping Adorable Cupcake Soaps
Advanced Soapmaking: Wedding Soap Favors

Designing Each Class

Now that you have class ideas, you need to bring those ideas to life by creating and developing content, format, projects and handouts. You don't want to walk into the classroom on class day and not have a plan. I've done this before. It was chaos. I had a two-hour timeslot and only filled up about forty minutes of it. The class was discombobulated and the flow was horrid. *Planning is key to successful classes and workshops.* You will need to determine and create:

- Class Content: What the students learn in class.

- Class Format: How you deliver the class content.

- Class Projects: What the students make in class.

- Class Handout: A guide for the students to take home.

Let's discuss each in more detail.

Class Content

Class content is *what* students will learn during class. What topics will be discussed? What information will be shared?

The biggest mistake when preparing class content is including too little or too much information. You don't have to cram everything related to your craft into one class. On the opposite side of the coin, you don't want to have a shortage of class content making the class boring and too brief.

Another mistake easily made is to create content that does not match the ability level of your students. You want your students to be able to grasp what you are teaching during class and take it home to expand on it and learn more by practicing. You are teaching a foundation for them to grow.

Make a list of topics for each class. If you are having a hard time, the magic wand exercise (keep reading!) will help you visualize your class and create a list of topics. Practicing your class, as discussed later, will help you know if you have too little or too much content for one class.

Class Format

Old Chinese proverb:

"Tell me and I will forget.
Show me and I will remember.
Involve me and I will understand.
Step back and I will act."

Remember the story I told you about getting vegetables thrown at me? Though that didn't really happen, I probably deserved it. It taught me a lot about how I wanted to format my classes so that students would get the most out of the experience. I decided that my classes would be hands-on, providing students with the most amazing and fulfilling workshop that I could provide. Although I perform demos every now and then, I usually turn down teaching opportunities where the host will not allow me to teach hands-on classes. That's my style and the format that I'm most comfortable with. It is what I'm known for in the industry. If you take a workshop with Amanda of Lovin' Soap

Studio, you are guaranteed to get your hands dirty and go home with a suitcase full of soap!

Class format is *how* you will deliver your class content. There are typically three types of formats that you can choose from or combine to create your class.

- Lecture: A lecture style class involves the class content being delivered orally. The instructor stands in front of the class and teaches by speaking.

  If I were doing a lecture style soap class, I would *tell* the students how to make soap. I might use images in a PowerPoint presentation so they can at least see pictures of the process. This, in my opinion, would be quite boring and ineffective for crafters, artists and makers.

- Demo: A demo style class involves the instructor, or someone who is helping, demonstrating a technique or project.

  If I were to teach a demo style soapmaking class, I would be in front of the class making a batch of soap while they watched. Although this is more effective than giving a lecture, as a visual element has been added, it is still not the most effective way to teach a craft.

- Hands-on: A hands-on class involves the students actively participating in the class by making a class project based on the information given by the instructor. This hands-on element is what turns your classes into interactive workshops.

My soapmaking workshops are all completely hands-on. Each student gets to make a two-pound batch of soap to take home with him or her. This is the most effective way to teach a craft and one that students appreciate, value and have no problem spending their hard earned money on.

Which Format is Right for You?

It depends. I can say from experience that students want to get their hands dirty and do it themselves! My classes and workshops are known for their hands-on learning style. Each student gets to make a batch of soap from start to finish. They get to weigh each ingredient, learn to use a scale, make their own lye solution, pick out fragrances and colors, bring to trace, pour and take home their own batch of soap.

When I started teaching soapmaking classes, I noticed that most of the other classes I found online were teaching demo style classes or partial hands-on, where a large batch of soap was made by the teacher or by the group of students and then divided out among the students to color and pour into a small mold. I needed to find a way to make my classes stand out, so having a hands-on format in which students completely made their own batch of soap did the job.

Not only does a hands-on class create confidence in the process that you are teaching, *as nothing makes a student learn better than doing*, it adds value and puts you above those that are doing lecture or demo style classes only.

However, sometimes demo style classes, or even partial demo style classes are effective and can even be something you offer at a lower price than your hands-on classes.

For example, I took a simple glass blowing class. It was something I wanted to do for fun and knew I wasn't going to do again. We got to pick up the glass on our blowing stick, put it into the kiln and blow into it. The expert did the shaping, as that was something that we wouldn't be able to learn in the time allotted. This part demo/part hands-on class was perfect for this situation. A more detailed glass blowing class was offered for a higher fee for those that wanted to delve deeper into the craft and learn the shaping techniques. The shorter version was for those that were just a bit curious and wanted the experience.

I'll also occasionally teach ladies night groups where friends come to drink wine and make a batch of soap. They are there to have fun and socialize, so a detailed hands-on class probably isn't the best idea in this situation. I'll usually talk about the process, make the soap base and have them scent and color their own to take home. Half demo, half hands-on.

Figure out what will work best for you, for your students and for the craft that you're teaching.

The Class Project

What will students make in class? The class project is just that, a hands-on project that each student gets to complete during the workshop. Some examples from various crafts would be a batch of soap, a pincushion, a blouse, a knitted cap, a ceramic vase, a fused-glass pendant...etc.

Some Things to Consider:

- Time: Make sure the project you choose for students to complete in class *can* be completed in the time allowed. Nothing is more frustrating than not finishing a class project.

- Do-ability: Is the experience level of students compatible with the project? You don't want something so difficult that it will discourage students if they can't grasp the process under your instruction.

- Uniqueness: What makes your class project special or different? Is it more unique and interesting than similar classes? Try to be creative in coming up with your class project. If you were teaching sewing, would it be more popular to sew a pillowcase or an iPad cover? I'd want to make an iPad cover; I have enough pillowcases.

- Cost of Materials: You don't want a class project that is overly expensive to make, as that will translate to higher fees for your students. Choose projects that are cost effective for you as a teacher and also for the students who might want to reproduce the project at home. Make sure your class fee covers the cost of the materials.

Make up the class project ahead of time for two reasons:

1. You need samples for students to look at in class. Students love *ooing and ahhing* over what they're about to make. If your project has variations that the students can choose from, this helps them visualize the options and make their decision. For example, colors of glazes in pottery or fabric selections in

sewing shown ahead of time will give students a better visual of the final effect of their project.

2. You need samples to photograph for class registration website pages and for social media content.

Most people are visual. If you aren't the greatest photographer, I really recommend you get help taking stunning photographs of your class projects for marketing purposes. A horrible picture on your class website page can be a turn-off for potential students. The class project can make or break your class. A whiz-bang class project, with an awe-inspiring picture posted to the class registration website page will help to sell your class.

See if you can find a photographer that will trade you a photography session of your class samples for registration in your class!

The Class Handout

The handout I give students mirrors all of the things discussed in class and even includes the soap recipe and instructions so they can refer back to it if needed. Include things such as:

- Step-by-step instructions.

- Recipes and supply lists.

- References and resources that include suppliers and further reading materials.

My class handouts are detailed and serve as great reference guides. As an added income stream, you could even sell the handouts online as PDF downloads or eBooks for students who can't make your classes.

Write It Out — Magic Wand!

Once you've decided on the class content, format and project, write it out. This magic wand exercise is something I learned from my partner, Benjamin Aaron. It is a great exercise to use during any type of planning session.

Think about what you wanted to learn when you first got started and go from there. What class content, class format and class project would have allowed you to learn the techniques of your craft in the most efficient way? What would have made it fun and exciting for you? Think back to when you first started your craft and knew nothing.

Let's pretend I'm doing this exercise for the first time. Below is what my basic soapmaking class will look like. Just put your pen to paper and ramble, magic wand in hand! With a magic wand, anything is possible; there are *no* limits. You can write it out from the experience of being a student or of being the teacher. I wrote mine out from the perspective of being the teacher.

Magic Wand Exercise for Basic Soapmaking Class

Students walk into the classroom and gather around a table waiting for other students to arrive. While they're waiting, I get to know them by asking if they've made soap before, asking why they signed up and how they found my classes. I have samples of soap on the table that allows them to see what we'll be doing during class. Once all of the students get there, I have everyone sign in. I introduce myself and briefly have the students introduce themselves. Then we get started.

I start off with talking about why we would want to make our own soap. I explain to them how and why I started making soap. I talk about my experience in the industry and let them know that once they complete the class they'll be able to comfortably and confidently repeat the process on their own. Then I talk a bit about the history of soapmaking and traditional methods of making soap. I also explain the different types of soap and processes that you can use.

I talk about ingredients and different oil properties, fragrance and essential oils, colorants, equipment, molds and safety. I pass around samples of ingredients as I talk about them so they can see and smell. Once I finish the lecture part of the class it is time to do our project.

Step by step I walk the students through the process. Each student has a station with a scale and equipment to make soap. They gear up in goggles and gloves for safety. They weigh out the lye and water.... (You get the point. Write down everything that you'll do during the hands-on project.)

After we make soap I talk about cleanup. Then we talk about how to cut, cure and store the soap.

Then its question time! I limit this time to 30 minutes. Class ends with me pointing out my website information and email on the class handouts. I let the students know that I'll be sending out a questionnaire and follow up email and that I welcome questions and discussion from them. I thank the students for coming and tell them that they allow me to do what I love!

After writing out your ideal class, you can break it down into a list of topics to discuss and even assign times to keep yourself on track. Here is what my topic list might look like from the above magic wand exercise for a three-hour basic soapmaking class.

Topics and Timeline for Basic Soapmaking Class

Start	10:00 a.m.
Students sign in	
Students introduce themselves	10:10 a.m.
Start lecture	10:20 a.m.
Why do we make soap?	
Explain why and how I started	
History of soapmaking	
Various methods	
Basic ingredients	
Oil properties	
Scenting soap	
Coloring soap	
Additives	
Equipment/molds	
Safety	
Basic process	
Hands-on lab	11:00 a.m.
Make soap	
Cleanup	11:50 a.m.
Closing lecture	12:00 p.m.
Cutting, curing and storing	
Basic packaging	
Questions	12:30 p.m.
Class is over	1:00 p.m.

Practicing the Class

Practice makes perfect! Once you've designed a new class, invite a few friends or family members over and conduct a class run-through with them. Teach the practice class just as you would the regular class. You now have your list of topics and a rough time schedule. Practicing the class will help you:

- Firm up the class content: Did your content fit in the time allotted? Do you have too much or too little content? If you have too much content for the time allotted, you might find that you can break your initial class into two separate classes. If you have too little content, discuss more topics.

- Evaluate the do-ability of the class project: Were your test students able to complete the class project? Was it too easy or too difficult? Were your test students satisfied with what they made in class?

- See what content you might have missed: Did your test students have questions about something you did not address? You know your craft so intricately that something you deem to be common sense might not actually be so for someone new to the craft.

- See what additional supplies or equipment you might have missed: Did you forget about providing containers to rinse out brushes? Did you forget scissors to cut fabric?

Ask for feedback after you've conducted your test run and then modify the class based on the responses you receive. You might find that you have too much content for the time allotted, or that the class project is just too difficult for the experience level of the students that you're teaching. Be clear with your practice class attendees that you will expect feedback from them. You could even give them an evaluation sheet to fill out after the class.

Chapter 4: Every Teacher Needs a Classroom

Classroom Options

Many people start by teaching out of their home. This is okay when you are first starting out, but you'll soon grow out of this as you grow your business. Your home is the perfect place to practice teaching and to practice new class content, but I recommend finding a space outside of your home to teach. As a home-based teacher you will be inviting students, oftentimes strangers, into your home and there are safety, liability and privacy issues in doing so. If an accident or injury occurs without the proper insurance coverage, you could be liable for any and all damages and bills. So, check your homeowners policy before going forward.

If you don't already have a studio or appropriate space, here are some ideas:

- A local craft studio: My first spot in Austin, Texas was one of those paint-your-own-ceramics studios. It was perfect. They had a classroom separate from the main studio and floor, which had tables and chairs and comfortably sat about 14 people.

- An artist co-op: Some artist co-ops offer rental rooms for classes and events. The added bonus is that you can usually advertise with the co-op to help get student signups.

- A supply shop: A supplier is a great place to inquire about using their space. The first two places I taught in Dallas, Texas were local soap and candle suppliers. It worked well for both of us, as I brought in new students who would then purchase supplies. They actually provided the supplies for class, and hosted the classroom space as well.

- A community center: Community centers usually have rooms that you can rent for classes and events.

- A library: Just like community centers, libraries sometimes have rooms to rent.

- A conference room: Many businesses rent out conference rooms that would be perfect for certain crafts.

- A daycare, hair salon, restaurant or any business that might host your classes after normal business hours. Just make sure the location is suitable for your craft. You don't want to make papier-mâché on carpeted floors.

- Anywhere with a party room! Do an Internet search for local party rooms and you might find some interesting spots.

How Much Should Something like this Cost?

It depends. I've run across a few situations and scenarios and they varied greatly. Some examples:

- A fixed fee: I prefer to teach where I can pay a fixed fee to rent a space. Fees for rentals will vary depending on where the space is located. Fees might be hourly, daily or weekly. I rented a community center room in Dallas for $62 an hour. My rental in Austin, Texas at a ceramics studio was about $400 for a Friday, Saturday and Sunday. I found a place in Las Vegas, NV at $1200 for the same. Now Vegas definitely has pull for a destination bootcamp, which would probably bring in more students, warranting that price. A higher fee doesn't mean the venue wouldn't end up making your class, workshop or bootcamp profitable.

- A percentage of your revenue: Some spaces will take a percentage of your revenue or a percentage of each student's registration fee. Some spaces I've approached wanted as much as 50 percent of my revenue. That just wasn't the best option for me, but depending on your situation and craft, it could work.

Once you establish classes where you live, branch out if you want.

Think big! I have students who have travelled from all over the United States and even the United Kingdom to take workshops. Make your classes a destination and people will travel from anywhere. My most successful bootcamp city is Austin. It is a great vacation spot so students will bring the family, and while mom or dad is taking the class, the rest of the family is out playing.

Spread out into other cities and dwellings. Do you have family that lives in New York or Denver? Both are fun destinations and would be great for establishing classes. Having family or friends living where you might teach is great because then you have a place to stay, reducing travel costs, and a place to possibly ship supplies and equipment.

Always remember...everything is negotiable. Don't be afraid to negotiate for a better price, especially if you make it a regular event at a particular location. Ask if the proprietor or landlord will discount the price if you book once a month or a certain number of times during the year.

Classroom Requirements

What are the space and classroom requirements for your craft? Make a list of what your ideal rental will include. Do you require tiled or laminated floors, access to a kitchen, etc.? For soapmaking, my list of requirements includes:

List of Classroom Requirements

A sink with hot water to wash dishes.

A minimum of two electrical outlets to run the stick blenders.

Parking for students.

Private room with no access by public. I don't want random people walking into the class.

A door that locks overnight. I don't want to break down my classes overnight for multiple day bootcamps.

Wood, tile or laminate flooring (No carpet).

Questions to ask when looking at a potential classroom:

- Who provides the table and chairs?

- Does rental time include setup/take down?

- Where can students park?

- Is there a cancellation fee if you have to cancel the event?

- Is a deposit required?

- Are you provided a key or will you need to rely on someone to let you in? Make sure you have the individual's cell number and that you touch base with them the night before! I've had to wait at a facility for someone to come and unlock the door; it made my class start late.

Classroom Rental Contracts

Is a contract needed?

Yes! If the facility rents to others already, then they will probably have one in place for you to fill out. If they do not, make sure something is in place for the benefit of both parties. Can you imagine planning a workshop, getting to the facility and someone else is using it?

A contract is important for both parties, and specifies topics such as:

- The rental date and times.

- The price of the rental.

- Cancellation policies.

- Room capacity.

- Deposit policies.

- What's included? (Chairs, table, etc.)

- Cleanup procedures.

Insurance

Some rental facilities will require you to have your own insurance and provide a certificate of insurance. Since you are operating as a business, you should already have insurance in place to protect yourself. As an educator, I recommend professional liability as well. Here are some types of insurance that you could look into.

- Professional Liability Insurance: PLI, also called Errors & Omissions (E&O), insures you if a student is hurt or causes damage by using the advice, techniques or skills learned during your class.

- General Liability Insurance: This is insurance that protects you from a variety of claims that can arise from the operation of your business, including bodily injury for you and your students and property damage for your classroom rental.

At the time of this writing, my current insurance provider is K & K Insurance[1]. They offer a platform called *Instructor of the Arts*, which includes both general liability and professional liability.

If you are a soap or cosmetic maker, The Handcrafted Soap & Cosmetic Guild[2] and Indie Business Network[3] offer general liability insurance and an add-on for professional liability insurance.

Many other industry guilds or member-based organizations offer insurance or can recommend a place for you to start your search.

Insurance is important to have in our current litigious times. It is better to be safe than sorry.

What is Your Ideal Class Size?

Several factors will determine your ideal class size. If you conducted a practice run, you already have a good idea as to how many students you can teach at one time. Some things to consider:

---

[1] www.kandkinsurance.com/Recreation/Pages/Art-Instructor.aspx
[2] www.soapguild.org
[3] www.indiebusinessnetwork.net

Is your class format demo or hands-on? A demo style class might accommodate more students if it only involves their watching your demonstration. A hands-on class might be best with fewer students (6-12) so you can keep an eye on everyone and make sure they are creating the project correctly.

What is your space like? How many people can be comfortably accommodated in the room? How many tables and chairs do you have? One way to think more spatially and plan accordingly is the number of students per square foot. If you teach in an 800-square-foot facility and you have nine students (10 total including you), then each student might have about 80 square-feet to work with, depending on furniture and fixtures. Eighty square-feet might be overkill for sewing, but not near enough for sculpting.

How much parking is available? You'll want to make sure all of your students have available parking. Usually this is more of an issue in bigger cities like New York or Philadelphia or even in many downtown areas.

Does your project require any dangerous tools or chemicals? A smaller class size would be best so you can adequately supervise the students.

A smaller class size is always a great selling point! Smaller class size means more intimate interaction with a teacher, which provides value.

Teacher's Assistant

Consider the value of having an assistant or teacher's aide. Assistants can allow you to book bigger classes. Assistants should have the basic knowledge of what will occur in class so they can best help. Be clear with your assistants as to their role during classes. Are they to pass out supplies, wash dishes or assist students with their class project? How will you compensate them? Do they get the class for free or will you pay them a fee? All of these things need to be decided beforehand. Having a class assistant can be a valuable asset.

Amanda Gail

Chapter 5: Pricing Classes, Workshops & Webinars

Knowing how much to charge for teaching your craft can be a bit tricky. Craft classes vary in price and can range from $10 for a simple scrapbooking class, $49 for a sewing class to upwards of $300 for a stained glass or precious metal jewelry class. Prices will vary within your industry as well. One instructor might charge $49 for a sewing class and another $89 for a similar sewing class. Research what others are charging for similar classes. How do your classes compare in content and format?

If the class another instructor is teaching is demo only and you are going to be teaching a hands-on class, then you most certainly should charge more.

Are you teaching in a big city, a tourist type city or a remote suburb? Usually bigger cities or touristy cities can support higher prices for classes. I can charge more in Austin, Texas than I can in Caddo Mills, Texas.

When I first started teaching my own classes, I charged $69 per class. As I built up my teacher credibility and became more of an industry expert, I raised my prices. I now charge about $129 per class. We'll talk about building your teacher credibility later.

Once you determine a price, you'll need to determine the minimum number of students needed to 'make' the class. Take into consideration all of your expenses to see what the class or workshop will cost to produce. Expenses might include some of these items depending on your situation:

- Travel including airfare, gas, ground-transportation.

- Meals while traveling.

- Hotels.

- Rental car.

- Guest teacher fees.

- Travel for guest teachers.

- Classroom rental.

- Chair, table or equipment rental.

- Supplies for class projects.

- Snacks and drinks (if you provide in class).

- Marketing and advertising.

- Payment processing and credit card fees.

- Your minimum fee for teaching (pay yourself!).

Total everything to see where you end up. Here is an example of my expenses for a two-day bootcamp weekend with a guest teacher. Your expenses might vary greatly from mine, so just look at this as a general example.

Sample Soapmaking Bootcamp Weekend Expenses

Travel - gas to Austin from Dallas- $129
Meals - $100
Hotels - $120
Guest teacher fees - $300
Travel for guest teachers - $320
Classroom rental - $450
Supplies for class projects - $120
Snacks and drinks (if you provide in class) - $50
Marketing and advertising - $50
Payment processing and credit card fees - $39
Your minimum fee for teaching (pay yourself!) - $1000
Total estimated expenses - $2678

This is the minimum income I need to cover the expenses including my teaching fee. I charge about $446 per student for a four-class soapmaking bootcamp ($129 per class minus a four-class bundle discount. More on discounting later.) so I will need at least seven students enrolled for the bootcamp to be profitable. Anything over that is gravy!

Pricing Webinars

A webinar usually has drastically lower expenses. You can teach a webinar from your home and in your pajamas if you want! The biggest cost will be the software you use and, of course, your teaching fee. You might also consider sending out a kit so that during the webinar, students can create a class project based on the topics you are covering.

There are two schools of thought when pricing webinars.

1. Charge less because your expenses are less, giving students a cheaper option if they can't afford your regular classes.

2. Charge the same price as your regular classes, because your time and content is the same value whether delivered in person or online.

You might charge a bit less if there won't be a class project. Do whatever you can to have a class project if your craft can support it. A class project is still possible if you send out kits or if you require students to purchase supplies locally (such as needles and yarn for a knitting webinar). For example, if you teach a basic knitting class and charge $49 for the physical class, maybe you can charge $29 or $39 for the webinar version. You can give your students a required supply list so they have supplies ready for the online class.

For some crafts, it's not going to be possible to complete a class project during a webinar, such as craft welding, glass blowing or maybe even pottery. However, for some crafts it is possible, such as sewing, paper crafting or jewelry making. You know your craft well enough to make that decision.

Discounts

Everyone loves a discount! Consider some of these while structuring your pricing for classes and workshops.

- Early-bird registration discount: If students sign up before a given day, they receive a discount for signing up early. This is a great way to get registrations in a timely manner to make sure the class will make. Some students like to part with their money as close to the class date as possible, so by offering an incentive for signing up early, they are more likely to sign up during the early-bird pricing registration.

- Group discounts: If a group of friends all want to sign up for a class, consider giving a discount. It could be a percentage or simply a certain dollar amount off each registration. It's incentive for a potential student to find friends to take the class with them.

- Bootcamp discount: When I price my bootcamps and list them on my website I price each class individually, and then I have a bootcamp price for students who want to signup for the entire bootcamp. This gets students excited about signing up for the whole thing and not just for individual classes. For example, a four-class bootcamp price will look something like this:

Sample Soapmaking Bootcamp Weekend Pricing

Class 1 - $129
Class 2 - $129
Class 3 - $129
Class 4 - $129
Total $516
Bootcamp Price - $466 <- You save $50!
Early-bird Bootcamp Price - $446 <- You save $70!

I will create individual website cart pages for each class at $129 and one cart page for the bootcamp at $466. My website cart software allows for the cart item to be put on sale, so I will put the bootcamp cart item on sale for $446 until my early-bird pricing is over (usually four weeks before class). This way a student can sign up for any number of individual classes or for the entire bootcamp and get a nice discount.

ALWAYS spell out the value of your classes and workshops in your marketing and on your website.

My class is worth the price because:

- You will take home xxxx that they make in class, which has a retail value of xxxx.

- You will learn from an industry expert with xxxx number of years in the industry.

- The class is hands-on and the experience will give you the confidence to repeat the process at home on your own.

- You will go home with a detailed handout that you can refer back to again and again.

Don't underprice your classes. It is always easier to lower prices than to raise them. If you list your classes and you're not getting any signups, put them on sale or offer discounts. There is no absolute science to pricing, so it might take some trial and error to find your sweet price spot.

Your price is probably good if you have an enrollment rate of 70 percent or more. This means that if you have 16 spots available, you get at least 11 students enrolled. If you only get two or three students enrolled then either the price is way off or your marketing needs some work.

Creating Income Goals

Whether teaching is your sole source of income or you teach to bring in a bit of extra cash, creating goals and having a game plan to reach those goals is beneficial to make sure you earn the amount of money you desire.

You can break your income goals down into yearly goals, monthly goals, class registration goals, etc. For example, let's say that I want to earn at least $60,000 gross per year teaching classes. Let's break it down.

Monthly Income Target: $5,000 gross

My workshop fee per student is about $400 for a three-day workshop. I will need to sign up thirteen students to hit my goal of $5,000 each month.

Monthly Student Target: thirteen students signed up for a $400 workshop.

This $5,000 goal per month is a gross total, meaning this income amount is before taking out expenses, costs and taxes. The actual amount that I pocket will be less.

Let's pretend that you own an art studio and you want to bring in an extra $300 gross per month teaching painting classes. Your painting class is $69. That would mean that you need at least 5 students per month to make your $300 goal. What is your class signup maximum? If you can only teach three students per class, you will need to schedule two classes to meet your goal of five signups. If your class minimum is 10 students, then you will only need to schedule one class per month.

Chapter 6: Putting it all Together

Class Descriptions

Class website description pages are what sell your classes. They have all of the information needed for a potential student to make a decision to sign up or not. They need to be detailed, compelling and show value. A good class description page should include:

- An interesting and creative description of what students will be learning.

- A beautiful picture of the class project.

- Why they need to learn the craft.

- Why they need to learn it from you (and not someone else).

- Class location.

- Class time and date.

- What they need to bring.

- Value added items (handouts, etc.).

- Value of what they are making and taking home (retail value).

Be sure to use bold headings and bullet points for the important information, as people tend to pay more attention to those. For example, good website page content for my basic soapmaking class might look like this:

Basic Soapmaking: Learn to Make Your own Natural Handcrafted Soap!

What you put onto your body is just as important as what you put into your body. Using skin-loving ingredients such as shea butter, coconut oil, olive oil, natural essential oils and natural colorants, **you will get to make your own two-pound batch of soap to take home with you!** This hands-on class will give you the confidence to make soap in your home.

During class we will discuss:

- What soapmaking is.
- Why you would want to make our own.
- Equipment.
- Supplies.
- Ingredients.
- Safety.
- The basic process.
- A basic recipe.

During the hands-on portion of class you will get to:

- Select and blend your essential oils to fragrance your soap.
- Select your additives and coloring.
- Weigh out and make the lye solution.
- Weigh out the oils and additives.
- Mix your soap and pour into the mold.

You will make a two-pound batch of soap, the equivalent of about 8 bars, from start to finish - a retail value of $60.00!

Class location: 1234 Street, City, State, 64111

Date: Saturday, April 4, 2015

Time: 10 am - 1 pm

All supplies including base oils, essential oils, additives, colorants, equipment and molds will be provided. You will need to bring a pair of safety goggles and an apron.

Class size is limited so sign up quickly!

About the instructor:

[Insert bio here.]

Class Policies & Rules

There are several policies that you'll need to decide on in order to make things run smoothly during registration and classes.

Registration Policy

This sets the guidelines for where and how students can register. Do they register online or by email? Is full payment or a deposit due to secure their registration in your class?

Let's say a student calls and tells you that they will be in class. Does that count as a registration? They might believe they're registered and will bring cash or check on the class day. That might be okay with you, but I personally don't allow this practice. There are many downsides; they might not come if they orally commit and don't make a payment. My classes have a signup limit so I wouldn't want that spot to be wasted and leave someone out who really wants the spot.

Payment Policy

When is payment due? How can payment be made? Do you take installments? Do you take Paypal, cash, check and/or chocolate bars?

Refund/Cancellation Policy

This is a big one. What happens if a student wants to cancel her registration? If it's done months in advance, that's not a big deal, but what if three students cancel the day before class and you've already paid for the classroom rental, a guest teacher and more?! That's quite a hit to your bottom line. It is important to have a clearly defined refund/cancellation policy to determine if students can cancel, reschedule or receive refunds.

Classroom Policy

How are students expected to behave in class? Are cell phones allowed? Do they need to dress a certain way? Can they bring food? Can they bring their pet?

Here are my usual policies:

Sample Class Policies

Payment & Registration Policy:
Registration must be completed by filling out the online registration at www.yourwebsite.com. You can find a registration button on each individual class page or on the bootcamp page. During registration you will be directed to Paypal where you can pay for your class using your Paypal account or a credit/debit card. You don't have to have a Paypal account to make a payment.

Payment must be paid in full for your spot in class to be held.
No verbal or written requests serve to save you a spot in class so be sure to register online and make your payment!

Cancellation Policy:
You can cancel your spot in class for any reason UP TO four (4) weeks prior to class and receive a full refund minus an administrative fee of $10.00. You must submit your cancellation and refund request in writing by email to email@website.com within the time frame allotted.

If you cancel your spot in class WITHIN four (4) weeks prior to class, you will receive a class credit that is good towards future classes. No refund will be given. This is due to us having to pay rental facility charges, supply charges and teacher/speaker fees. You can

---

however transfer your class spot to another person as long as you notify me in writing by email to email@website.com prior to class.

If you don't show up for class without any notice you will NOT receive a refund or class credit for future classes.

If we have to cancel the class for any reason, you will receive a full refund.

Class Policies:
You must be 18 years or older to participate in classes unless otherwise specified in the class description.

Please do not bring children or pets to class.

Cell phones need to be on silent or vibrate during class. If you need to take a call, please step outside of the classroom.

Feel free to take pictures during class! We're not camera shy!

Scheduling Classes & Workshops

When should you schedule classes? Weekends, mornings, once a week, once a month...?

This will vary by the industry and location as well as by the season. Some general rules to follow:

Weekends and weeknights are often best, as most people with expendable income work during the day. 'Most' people get off work at 5 p.m., so classes that start at 6 or 7 p.m. do well and 'most' people want to sleep in on the weekends so classes that start at 9 or 10 a.m. do well.

Don't book classes on a holiday or even weekends that surround a holiday. People aren't typically going to give up a holiday to take a class and often are out of town or have guests right before or after holidays. With that said, you can tailor classes to groups and even market them for fun family holiday parties or gift making sessions.

The beginning and ending of the school year is usually slower as parents are focused on getting their kids ready for school or getting them adjusted to the summer. However, end of school time could be great for kid's classes.

Kids classes during the summer are best if booked during the day as parents and caretakers are always looking for fun ways to spend summer days.

Private classes can be booked at any time since your student will dictate when they are available. I usually ask for best times/dates and see how our schedules mesh.

How to Handle Class Registrations

Once you have your classes scheduled, you'll need to then determine how to take registrations for.

All you'll need is a website with a shopping cart. I personally use Wordpress[4] to provide content management for my website and I used a plugin called Woo Commerce[5], which is a shopping cart

---

[4] www.wordpress.com
[5] www.woocommerce.com

application. The cart runs payments through Paypal[6] to process debit and credit cards.

There are other software applications and services you can purchase to handle registrations, but I've found that having a Wordpress site with Woo Commerce works best and is easiest for me to maintain. I am a do-it-yourself type of person and all three of these applications are wondrously easy for me to learn and use for my business.

If you don't feel confident in setting up a website yourself, you can find someone to help you build it for a fee. Let them know the purpose of your website and how you'll be using it.

---

[6] www.paypal.com

Basic Soapmaking Class in Dallas, TX - I rented a community center to conduct classes.

Class in Austin, TX

A student hard at work swirling soap.

Chapter 7: Finding Your Students

If you build it, will they come? Yes! But it will take some work.

Now that you've got everything ready to go, you need people to sign up to take your classes! Just having a website does not guarantee that students will magically find you. Here are some ways to find your students:

- Post on Craigslist[7]. Craigslist has a community and class section.

- Post a flyer at local artist co-ops and make sure you ask if they can add it to their website or post it on their social media page(s).

---

[7] www.craigslist.org

- Post a flyer at local suppliers or craft shops and request they post it online for you.

- See if your industry has a member-based guild or organization. Our guild, the HSCG, actually has a class-listing page by state, which makes it easy for students to find classes.

- Post flyers at local coffee shops, community centers, stores, schools or any place that will allow you to post a flyer.

- Word of mouth! Tell all of your family and friends to help spread the word. Post on your personal social media sites, such as Facebook and Twitter.

Creating a Community

A community can often be described as a social group sharing common characteristics or interests. Creating a community of students, potential students, suppliers, guest teachers and anyone else associated with your craft is important to recurrently attain more registrations and build a social foundation around your teaching. Remember my comment regarding creating a series of classes for your craft?

By building your community, you are creating a pool of dedicated and engaged students who will sign up for your classes!

Over the last several years I have built a community around my craft, soapmaking. This community takes my classes, purchases books and eBooks, purchases consulting services and hangs out on my blog to discuss issues, learn from my tutorials and engage in community based behaviors. My major platform is my blog at Lovinsoap.com. I get an average of 2,000-2,200 website hits a day, and it is continually growing. Here's how I did it.

In order to get, you must give! This is true for any business. I *give* by publishing free tutorials, soapmaking advice, articles, troubleshooting pages and resource pages for my industry. I have created a community of soapmakers who are thirsty for knowledge, advice and how-to's. This community responds by taking classes, purchasing eBooks, published books and consultation services that I offer. If you teach a craft, follow my simple recipe for building your own community.

- Step 1: Get a website URL and hosting service. The website URL can be your business name, your name or something related to your craft.

- Step 2: Install your blogging software. My personal favorite is Wordpress. Most website hosts have a button to install Wordpress through the hosting console.

- Step 3: Start publishing articles about your craft. It could be articles about how to get started, basic ingredients, suppliers that you like...anything!

- Step 4: Publish free tutorials. My blog features tutorials from the basics of soapmaking to advanced swirling and design techniques. People love how-to's and recipes. Be sure to post pictures of the steps and the final project.

- Step 5: Conduct interviews! People love to share their stories and to be featured. Once published, they will then send all of their family and friends over, which will potentially give you more publicity and you might even gain some new followers.

- Step 6: Post class pictures. Anytime you have a class, post some pictures from the event, and at the end of the post, list the upcoming classes with links so people can sign up. Make sure your class pictures are exciting. Get students in action and get shots of their finished projects.

- Step 7: Post interviews from students who now have a successful business doing their craft. This shows people the value of taking one of your classes as it provided another crafter a good foundation to get going.

Always answer blog comments and questions to keep the dialogue open and reciprocal. If your audience doesn't think they are being heard, they will likely quit talking.

Sign up for social media sites such as Facebook, Twitter, Instagram and Pinterest! Many of the things posted on your blog will be summarized and posted to your social media sites with links back to your blog.

Your community will support you by signing up for classes, buying books and even signing up for other services that you might offer!

Soapmaking Bootcamp in Austin, TX - A variety of soap was made by each student.

Soapmaking Bootcamp in Austin, TX - Students are measuring their ingredients.

Chapter 8: Collaboration

Collaboration is a great way to boost the popularity and exposure of your classes and workshops. Collaboration is also a great way to lose your ass, get sued, ruin your reputation and lose trust from your students. This section is important. Read it twice.

Imagine that you teach sewing classes. Your best friend sews as well. You go over to her house and see that she's sewn this adorable tooth fairy pillow. You think it would be the perfect project for a sewing class. Better yet, your friend could just teach it! How fun would that be? You'll teach how to sew an iPod cover and she'll teach how to sew the tooth fairy pillow.

You get the workshop listed on the website and students start to enroll. You do all of the promotion, handle the registrations, pay the credit card processing fees, pay the rental and supply fees and handle all of the business.

Class time comes and a few wonky things occur.

You end up with a few extra students because your friend told a few of her friends that they could just show up and didn't need to register like everyone else. You don't have enough project supplies for everyone, as they weren't on your roster.

Your friend starts teaching her part of the workshop and although you've allowed one hour, she's done in ten minutes and isn't really that great of a teacher.

Its time to divvy up the money and your friend demands half of all the fees collected, because, of course, she taught half of the workshop. You never took the time to explain all of the expenses and to discuss how money would be divided.

All hell breaks loose because of these issues and now your friendship is in jeopardy.

Lessons learned?

Make sure your co-instructor follows all of your policies and procedures.

Make sure your co-instructor is a good teacher! Does she already teach classes? Take one and see if your style will mesh with her style. If she is new, ask that she conduct a practice class so you can witness her methods and style.

Make sure all money matters, especially the payment of a teacher fee or division of revenue, are agreed upon ahead of time.

Collaboration with Other Instructors

Collaboration with other teachers can bring attention, exposure and varied-classes to your workshops. This can open you up to new students and new exposure. If you collaborate with other teachers, there are some things to figure out, agree upon and get in writing.

There are many considerations when deciding percentages and payouts for guest instructors, including:

- Who is receiving the registrations for the classes? This usually means that this person is handling the web costs, payment processing costs, etc.

- Who is doing the marketing and advertising?

- Who is paying the rental and insurance?

- Who is paying for travel expenses?

- Who is paying for supplies?

- Popularity of the guest teachers. Is your guest teacher an expert in the industry or someone new to the industry and unknown to potential students? More expert and big name speakers will require a higher speaker fee or higher percentage of revenue generated. Their name will draw in the students though, so keep that in mind.

It is common for one person to have more expenses than the other, so take a good look at all expenses and efforts being brought to the table by both parties. Write it all down and discuss to reach an agreed upon deal that is fair to both parties. You can setup your percentages and payouts however you want. But it is extremely important that things are clearly defined and established before you start taking registrations for a collaborative workshop or class.

I've taught with several others and here are some sample deals that I've been a part of.

- Percentage of class income + travel allowance: The host pays for all travel (airfare or mileage and hotel) for an *agreed upon maximum amount* (you don't want to pay for first class tickets!). The host will then pay the guest teacher a percentage of class revenue. This is great for motivating the guest teacher to help advertise and market the class. The more signups there are, the more money in each of your pockets!

- Percentage of class income: Same as above, but the guest teacher pays for their own travel. In this scenario the percentage that the guest teacher receives might be a bit higher in order to cover travel costs.

- Teaching fee + travel allowance: The host pays for all travel and pays a one time agreed upon fee. The guest teacher will not make more than the agreed upon fee, therefore it might not motivate them to help acquire signups and do their share of publicity for the event. If you're filling up classes on your own...no big deal. But if you're new and need help with publicizing classes, you might want to consider a percentage.

Collaboration with Suppliers

I've collaborated with suppliers to offer my students free supplies, coupons for supplies or even a door prize at bootcamps (a soap mold or soaping oils). This puts the supplier's name in front of new people to gain new business and it provides value to my bootcamps by offering free stuff, prizes and coupons! Sometimes I will put the supplier as a sponsor on the website or in marketing materials. Just be sure to work out all of the details prior to publicizing the collaboration.

Just ask! Email suppliers and tell them about yourself and your classes and workshops. Ask if they'd be interested in sponsoring a workshop in return for a mention on Facebook, their logo on your website or some other publicity that you can offer.

Soapmaking Bootcamp in Austin, TX

Basic Soapmaking Class in Dallas, TX

Chapter 8: Teaching Your Craft

Before the Class

One month before classes, make a list of supplies needed and make sure that everything is ordered and gets to you in time for classes. If you have specialty items or long lead-time supplies, do this even earlier. Make a list of equipment that you'll need and make sure you have the entire assembly of equipment ready to go. Does anything need to be cleaned or put together?

Two weeks before class touch base with the rental space owner to make sure everything is on track and ready for your rental. Stuff happens. Sometimes you can be left off of a calendar and the space gets double booked or the business might not even be in business anymore!

(A stretch, but prepare for anything.) Don't show up at your rental space the day of class without having contacted the person in charge.

One week before class print out class handouts so they are ready to go. Send out an email reminder and include any important information that the students need to know to prepare. This includes the following:

- Class location: Provide the physical address of where the class will take place. You could even include a link to Google maps. If the venue has a phone number, provide that as well, so if they need to call for directions the morning of class, they can call the venue instead of your cell phone (you're preparing for class!).

- Items the students need to bring: If the class requires the students to bring anything, be sure to remind them in this email. It should have also been on the class description website page so it shouldn't be a surprise a week before class. My soapmaking classes require students to bring safety goggles, so I make sure to include that and mention where they can be purchased.

- Items the students should not bring: This might seem a little silly, but I always include a line that says something like, "Please do not bring other people, kids and pets." You would be surprised what some people try to bring to class.

Here is my typical email — informal, short and sweet.

Hello future soapmakers! This Saturday (09/22) is the beginner Soapmaking Class!

Class starts promptly at 1:30 and lasts about two hours. Please allow for an extra half hour in case we go over a bit...we have a full class!

Please bring: Safety Goggles (you can purchase from hardware stores). Wear clothes you don't mind getting dirty and wear closed toed shoes. I'll have a class handout for you so bring a pen or pencil in case you want to take notes. Feel free to bring a drink or snack.

Please DO NOT bring: Children, other people...pets.

Class Location: Austin Art Studio, 123 Austin St, Austin, Texas 78098 | 555.555.5555

My cell is 555-555.5555 - feel free to call or text. My phone is turned off 30 minutes before class so if you are running late or are lost; please call Austin Art Studio for directions.

Please let me know if you have any questions! I'll see you on Saturday!

-Amanda Gail

During the Class

Introduce yourself to each student as they walk in. Get to know each student individually during the class. Address students by their name. Have your students wear nametags. This will help them get acquainted with each other as well as you.

Start class on time. You might have some stragglers. I have waited 5 minutes past a class start time, but anything over that isn't fair to those that arrived on time. Latecomers can be caught up at moments available during the class. I've observed when a late arriver shows up, it's the students sitting next to that person that step up and catch that person up to speed by pointing out the page number of the handout or helping them measure out the oil for their soap. We've all been late. It happens.

Let students take video and pictures. I know some teachers who are against students taking videos and pictures during classes and this topic can be a bit controversial. Why? This is free advertising. Should a student video the whole class? No. But is it okay for a student to video a soap swirling technique or how to sew a certain stitch? Sure! They might even post it on their blog or social media outlet and it could turn into free advertising! You'll have people talking about how much fun they had and what they learned.

After the Class

Thank each student. As each student leaves, thank him or her for coming. If you taught a class project, ask them how their project turned out. If you notice something cool about the project, point it out! "Brenda, I love your color scheme!"

Send a follow-up email. I usually wait about a week and then send out a follow-up email. I thank the student for attending the class again and include things like:

- Feedback request: Survey Monkey[8] is a great (and free) resource for creating a feedback form that you can send to students. Include a link to the form in your follow-up email. You

---

[8] www.surveymonkey.com

can ask whatever questions you want, but I've found that these two fill-in-the-blank statements are most effective.

The most valuable part of this workshop was:

_____

This workshop would've been more effective if:

_____

People tend to ignore surveys with tons of questions. They just don't have the time.

- Support documents: Many times I mention to the students that I will send them the recipe sheet in digital format or something similar. Include any digital handouts or documents as needed.

- Resource links: Often I mention resources that I forgot to include in my handout. It could be a website, a blog or a supplier that is new. Include links to resources that you mentioned during class.

- Upcoming class schedule: Be sure to include your upcoming classes or a link to your classes on your website. If they loved your class, they'll sign up for more or at least bookmark it for future reference.

Assessments & Certificates

Consider offering certificates for students who take classes. They can be certificates of completion or certificates for levels of accomplishment.

Certificates of completion are pretty straightforward. Students take your class, and upon completion, they receive a certificate.

You could also offer certificates for passing an assessment for various levels of your craft. The assessment could test the students on practical skills and their comprehension of the craft. So for example, I could offer assessments for students to be certified as a Basic Soapmaker, Intermediate Soapmaker and Master Soapmaker. Each assessment would include a practical part and a written comprehension part. The practical part would involve the student making a batch of soap of various levels. The written comprehension part would have questions pertaining to the level of certification.

How to Handle Troublesome Students

I almost didn't include this section in the book, and I'm certainly not an expert, but I wanted to mention it, as it's such a big part of teaching. There are websites, books and videos dedicated to handling your class. I would recommend reviewing the subject before you're faced with a situation that you are not prepared for.

Here are some possible troublesome scenarios that might pop up and how to best handle them.

The Student Who Wants to Teach Your Class for You

I get this one quite often. Many times there are students who sign up for my basic soapmaking class who have a bit of experience making soap; perhaps they've made one batch of soap or read an outdated book. Oftentimes the person doing this is giving misinformation or information that simply contradicts my standard curriculum.

I usually respond with a recognition of the fact they have some knowledge on the topic, but ask that they pay attention and let those around them pay attention as my directions might differ from what they've been taught. If they are confrontational, present the chocolate cake analogy. Just as there is more than one way to bake a chocolate cake, there is more than one way to make a batch of soap. Gather different techniques and you'll soon have your own style of soapmaking.

The Student Who Talks Off Topic

You will likely run across one or more of these. The biggest problem with this is that they take time away from the topic being taught to talk about their Aunt Margaret or the troubles that their child is having in school.

NIP IT IN THE BUD. EARLY.

Your students paid for this class and they don't want to discuss Aunt Margaret when they signed up to talk about soap! Usually the people that do this, and do it in the worst possible way, don't realize they are being disruptive.

For example, you ask something like, "What is your favorite essential oil to use in soap?" and the student responds with, "Lavender! It is great for calming down before bedtime. I used some last night when I got a phone call from my Aunt Margaret. She said that she had paid the electricity bill twice and wasn't sure how to go about getting one of the payments back. I explained to her that they will just credit it...but she's such a worry wart. Just the other day she called to let me know that her cell phone was lost and if we need to get in touch with her we would need to just call her on her home phone. Next weekend is her birthday, so I thought I might get her a cell phone. We're trying to figure out if we'll have chicken tikka masala or stuffed goose with raspberry sauce for dinner. What does everyone here prefer?"

Screeeeee-atchhhhhhhhhh

I usually interrupt nicely, with "Excuse me, Carl...thank you for your thoughts" and then address the class with something like, "Let's move on because we have limited time together to cover everything that needs to be covered."

And without taking a breath start your next sentence, "Olive oil in soap creates a mild..." or "We can finish this discussion after class, but let's move on for the sake of time."

Just keep the class moving.

The Student who Jumps Topics

This is very important. You can count on getting a student in every class who is excited to learn and has many questions about the craft that you're teaching. You will be discussing a particular topic, for example base oils in soap, only to have them raise their hand and ask about scenting soap, a topic to be covered later in class.

You don't have to answer the off-topic question as it can derail the flow of your class. It is easy to get flustered, because you feel it is your duty to answer it right then. Let them know you appreciate their interest and enthusiasm without cutting them off.

You can respond with something like, "We are almost to that part of class and you will learn every way to scent soap. Let's finish this discussion on base oils first."

After I end a section of discussion, I ask if there are any questions about what we have discussed so far to try and stave off any questions about content yet to be covered. *I try not to say, 'Are there any questions?' as that leaves it open to ANY questions about anything.*

If you have a disruptive student, pull them aside and privately discuss the issues that are occurring. Never embarrass a student by calling them out in front of everyone.

Special Situations

It was 9:05 on a Saturday morning and even though I had one student absent, it was time to get started. I went into my intro and started getting to know the students. We started talking about why we wanted to make our own soap and I was going around the room to each student.

Suddenly, through the glass doors in the front of the building, I saw a young woman walk up the stairs. She fumbled a bit getting up the stairs and through the doors. I think my mouth dropped open a bit because she was getting around with the use of a white cane! It turns out she was legally blind. She didn't tell me ahead of time.

My initial thought, which I'm a bit ashamed of, was how on earth is a blind student going to make soap! Soapmaking requires using a scale, measuring ingredients and seeing the soap emulsify. And then I quickly said to myself, okay let's make it work. I sat her near the front so I could help her measure and do things that she might not be able to.

As she was sitting down, she flashed me a bright smile and said, "Sorry I didn't tell you ahead of time that I was legally blind." There was a bit of mischief in the statement, almost as if she was challenging me in a way. I told her that if she needed help with any of the hands-on portion of the class to just ask and I'd jump over there to help.

It turned out that she could see enough to use the scale but needed help with pouring and measuring as her depth perception was off. If I wasn't available to help her, her table buddy ended up being more than happy to help as needed. She really enjoyed the class and the experience as a whole.

Another time, I had a wheelchair bound student take a class. The class setup I was teaching only offered high tables that you worked at while standing. So if you were sitting in a folding chair, or a wheel chair, you couldn't see or get to everything on the high tables.

We made the best of it, and she didn't seem to mind at all when we placed some of the equipment on a stool within her reach. But it still wasn't ideal. In retrospect, we could have had a folding table that would make everything accessible to her.

I'm sharing these stories because I learned the importance of making my classes accessible to everyone. If someone comes in that has special needs, I'm prepared to make modifications to the class or process. My mental attitude is such that we will make anything work.

So, as you're preparing your space and thinking about your classes, have an action plan to accommodate situations such as these, as they are sure to happen every now and then. *Never should a student receive an inferior experience from a class you are teaching.* Be flexible and prepared, no matter their special situation.

You could even have a section on your signup form that asks if the student registering has a need for special accommodations.

Swirling Soapmaking Class in Austin, TX - My most popular class.

An army of student-designed soap.

A student hard at work swirling soap.

Chapter 10: Sell Yourself

How to Build your Teacher Credentials

Your teacher credentials *or cred* can include anything that indicates you are suitable to teach, such as teaching experience, speaking experience, practical experience, publications, training and certifications.

Why should people sign up for YOUR classes? Why should people spend their hard earned money to learn the craft from you?

You're probably not the only person teaching your craft. You will need to make yourself stand out and demonstrate your success and ability as a teacher by showcasing your teacher cred. If you don't have much cred, no worries, you can build it.

Teaching Experience

How many years have you been teaching? Where do you teach? How many students do you teach annually? If you are new to teaching, your teaching experience will obviously build the longer you teach. Showcase other credentials that you might have that make you qualified to teach, such as practical experience.

Speaking Experience

Most industries have conferences and trade shows. Most of these events have classes for attendees or speakers who give presentations on industry topics. Become an industry speaker. Most websites for these events have submission forms where you can submit your info and topic information. You could even create your own speaking events in your town to build a foundation for you as a speaker. Here is an example:

Give a Demo: Partner with a local studio or craft shop (or anywhere else you can find) and give a free demo of your craft. Talk about your craft's history, show examples of your work and demonstrate a quick technique or two. As a soapmaker, I have given demos for various groups including a homeschool group, a historical society and local suppliers.

Practical Experience

Maybe you haven't been teaching for very long, but the experience you have in actually making your craft is very valuable to your teacher cred. How many years have you been sewing, knitting, making candles, painting, etc.? Do you have a business selling your items? Most students aren't going to take a teacher seriously if they don't have practical experience in the craft they are teaching. If you are teaching a certain craft, obviously you have practical experience. Be sure to highlight that in your teacher cred.

Publications

Have you published anything related to your craft? This could even include your blog or articles submitted to other industry blogs. If you haven't, publishing articles and tutorials is a great way to build cred in your industry. Publish your own blog or submit articles to other industry blogs and publications. Be sure to highlight your publications using links on your website or blog.

For example, my industry, handcrafted soap, has three major industry publications, *Saponifier, Soap Collaborative and Handmade Magazine*. I've written for all of them. I publish my own blog, Lovinsoap.com and have written guests posts for other industry blogs including a popular industry blog, Soapqueen.com.

Training

Have you had any formal training in your craft? Did you go to art school? Have you completed workshops or attended seminars? Training is valuable, especially if the training was done with industry experts and leaders.

Certifications

I am a soapmaker and we have an industry guild, Soapguild.org. They offer certifications for soapmakers. Check out your industry and see if there are any certifications that you can get in your trade or craft.

Make a list! Write out your credentials. These will be used in your bio, on your website and in the marketing and branding of your classes.

Your Bio

A bio is oftentimes your sales pitch. It showcases some of your teacher cred from above and quickly lets students know that you're the right teacher. You should have your bio on your website and provide it to others, if you are teaching for someone else, so they can put it on their website.

There are many ways to write a bio, but if you're having trouble, here is what I suggest.

Open with a statement of what you teach.

BAH: Amanda Gail teaches soapmaking classes.

SUPER: Amanda Gail teaches students how to create handcrafted soap and body products. She teaches everything from the basics of soapmaking and body care products to advanced formulations, mold making, color and design techniques.

Throw in some of your teacher cred.

BAH: Amanda has been teaching for six years.

SUPER: Amanda has taught soapmaking at bootcamps and conferences all over the country, educating hundreds of students over the years. She is founder and co-director of a not-for-profit, Lovin' Soap Project, and currently teaches soapmaking to women in Haiti and Uganda. She has given presentations for the Handcrafted Soap and Cosmetics Guild, Central Soapers Workshop, Alabama Soap Conference, Tennessee Soap and Candle Meeting and the Texas Lonestar Soap and Toiletries Seminar. Amanda writes industry articles and tutorials she publishes on her blog, lovinsoap.com and is a guest writer for industry publications including *Saponifier, Handmade Magazine* and *Soap Collaborative.*

Throw in a bit about why your classes are special and unique.

BAH: Amanda's classes are hands-on and super fun.

SUPER: Amanda's popular hands-on style of classes provide students a safe and supervised environment to learn this artisan, trendy craft and the confidence to make soap and body care products on their own following the class.

Throw in something personal or fun to end.

BAH: Amanda lives in Kansas City.

SUPER: When not mixing oils and lye, Amanda enjoys travel, writing and morning coffee with her guy.

Let's put it all together!

Amanda Gail teaches students how to create handcrafted soap and body products. She teaches everything from the basics of soapmaking and body care products to advanced formulations, mold making, color and design techniques.

Amanda has taught soapmaking all over the country at bootcamps and conferences teaching hundreds of students over the years. She is founder and co-director of a not-for-profit, Lovin' Soap Project, and teaches soapmaking to women in Haiti and Uganda. She has been a speaker for the Handcrafted Soapmakers Guild, Central Soapers Workshop, Alabama Soap Conference, Tennessee Soap and Candle Meeting and the Texas Lonestar Soap and Toiletries Seminar. Amanda writes industry articles and tutorials she publishes on her blog, lovinsoap.com and is a guest writer for industry publications including *Saponifier, Handmade Magazine* and *Soap Collaborative*.

Amanda's popular hands-on style of classes provides students a safe and supervised environment to learn this artisan, trendy craft and the confidence to make soap and body care products on their own following the class.

When not mixing oils and lye, Amanda enjoys travel, writing and morning coffee with her guy.

It's a good start! Your bio will change depending on what you're using it for. Sometimes you might need to beef it up a bit and add more content. And sometimes you'll need to make it a bit shorter, perhaps for a handout or for an article signature. Create a couple of different versions so you'll have them on hand when needed.

Your Headshot

You need a headshot. You are a professional service provider, business owner and instructor and you need a headshot for your website and for other promotional opportunities. As a teacher, you are selling yourself. A headshot puts a face to your services.

You can take your own headshot, but if photography isn't your thing, get some professional help. It's worth paying a few extra dollars to get a professional headshot.

Does your headshot have to be stuffy and on a white or grey background? Heck no! We're crafters, not lawyers. You can be creative. Since you are promoting yourself and your craft, in addition to your regular headshot, you could even have a headshot taken of you doing your craft. It doesn't hurt to have several versions of a headshot for various uses.

HAPI Soapmakers in Mizak, Haiti (www.haitianartisans.com).

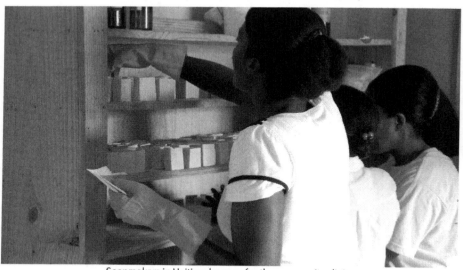

Soapmakers in Haiti make soap for the community clinic.

Chapter II: Setting up Your Business

The best resource to get information about setting up a business is the U.S. Small Business Administration website. You can find it at www.sba.gov[9] and find links to your state's website.

Choosing a Business Structure

You first need to determine the legal structure of your business. You'll have a few options, which come with various tax and legal implications. Two structures that I recommend when starting out are Sole Proprietorship and Limited Liability Company. There is also General Partnership, Limited Liability Partnership, S-Corporation and C-Corporation. I've only established my business as a Sole Proprietorship

---

[9] www.sba.gov

and a Limited Liability Company so I will discuss those. Before you setup your business, do your research at www.sba.gov or consult an expert, such as a lawyer or accountant, to help you decide on the right legal structure to fit your circumstances.

Sole Proprietorship

In a sole proprietorship, you own the company and are solely responsible for assets and liabilities. Most instructors start out as sole proprietors. Your taxes are filed on your personal income tax filing with no distinction between you and the business. You do not have to take any action to form a sole proprietorship; if you are actively teaching, bringing in money and acting in business activities, you are already a sole proprietor.

Although you don't need to register your business, you do need to obtain any necessary licenses or permits required by your state and city. Your local www.sba.gov website will have more information on what is required.

Typically a sole proprietorship's legal name is your legal name (e.g. Amanda Griffin). If your business will have another name (e.g. Lovin' Soap Studio), then you will need to register a DBA (doing business as) also referred to as a fictitious name or assumed business name. You will need to register a DBA in order to open a bank account and do business, write and receive checks under your fictitious name.

There is no distinction between you and your business. You report your income and expenses as part of your personal tax return on a Schedule C tax form.

Be aware that if you operate as a sole proprietor, you are personally responsible for your company's liabilities, including debts and legal claims filed against you, putting your personal assets at risk.

Limited Liability Company

In a limited liability company, your taxes are filed on your personal income tax filing with no distinction between you and the business. As the name suggests, you are protected from personal liability for debts or legal claims filed against you, but your personal assets are usually exempt.

To set up your LLC, you must file articles of organization with your state. Requirements vary by state, so check out your local www.sba.gov website for filing links and more information.

A LLC's legal name is the name you used when setting up your LLC (e.g. Lovin' Soap Studio). You won't need to register a DBA unless you will be doing business under another name besides your original filing name, (e.g. if I published books and wanted to use Lovin' Soap Publishing, I could file a DBA for that under Lovin' Soap Studio).

There is no distinction between you and your business if you have filed as a single-member LLC without electing corporate taxation. You report your income and expenses as part of your personal tax return on a Schedule C tax form.

Is Your Guest Teacher an Employee or Contractor?

This is another super important topic to consider. And again, since I'm no expert, consult a tax attorney about your specific situation and arrangements with guest teachers.

You can hire a guest teacher as either an employee or as an independent contractor. The facts of the teaching situation determine the status, not your preference or the preference of the guest teacher.

If you control the class content, curriculum, class format or if you require your teacher to go through certain training then your guest teacher should be classified as an employee. If your teacher has a regularly occurring schedule, she might be considered an employee. You must withhold and pay social security, Medicare and unemployment (FUTA) taxes based on their wages. You must also get a W-4 filled out by the employee and provide the employee with a W-2, filing copies with the Social Security Administration.

If your guest teacher handles class content, curriculum, class format and other aspects of the class, then your guest teacher is probably classified as an independent contractor. If your guest teacher is temporary or only teaches on an occasional basis, then she is probably classified as an independent contractor. An independent contractor is responsible for paying his or her own taxes. You do not withhold any taxes from their pay. You will be required to give her Form 1099-Misc and file a copy with the Social Security Administration.

For example, if you have Holly Port teach a liquid soapmaking class and you specify to her the process, the supplies and the curriculum that she is to use, then she is an employee.

If you have Holly Port teach a liquid soapmaking class and leave all of the details up to her — dates, times, length of class — then she is probably an independent contractor.

To be sure, consult a tax attorney.

You can also read the following publication from the IRS.

http://www.irs.gov/pub/irs-pdf/p1779.pdf

http://www.irs.gov/taxtopics/tc762.html

Accounting

As a business you will need to track your income and expenses. You can do this by using a spreadsheet or you can use a software program for accounting such as QuickBooks.

Because entire books are written on accounting (and I highly recommend that you read some), I'm not going to go into detail in this basic book. I recommend that you hire the help of an accountant or take accounting classes to get you started if you don't have any knowledge of accounting. Many cities have small business classes at community centers and colleges that you could take.

Every dollar that you collect needs to be accounted for and every expense needs to be recorded, as expenses reduce your taxable income. Taxes will need to be paid on your income based on your business structure. An accountant can help determine which tax documents need to be filed (there are usually both state and federal) and when.

Teaching soapmaking in Haiti to OFDALAF in Port-au-Prince (www.ofeda.com).

Pouring soap in Haiti.

Chapter 12: Liability, Environment and Procedures

If you skimmed the section on insurance, go back and read it again. You should have both professional liability insurance and general liability insurance.

How else can you protect yourself as an instructor?

Release of Liability Form

Obtain a release of liability form from each student. Make it a requirement to have it filled out, signed and collected before class starts. Because we use sodium hydroxide (lye) in soapmaking classes, I have students fill out a release of liability form and sign a lye safety statement. You should work with a lawyer to write your own form, but to give you an example, here is what mine looks like.

*This is provided for educational purposes only and should not be used without consulting your attorney.

Lovin' Soap Studio - Release of Liability and Lye Safety Statement*

I, _____, in consideration of my participation in the class, Basic Soapmaking, on this date; _____, 2015, in Kansas City, MO, hereby release Amanda Griffin, the owner of Lovin' Soap Studio and employees and agents, and any other people officially connected with this event, from any and all liability for damage to or loss of personal property, sickness or injury from whatever source, legal entanglements, imprisonment, death, or loss of money, which might occur while participating in this event. Specifically, I release said persons from any liability or responsibility for my physical condition, and for the presence or actions of any other participants. I am aware of the risks of participation, which include, but are not limited to, cuts, burns, or other soap making related injuries, though rare, which could occur. I understand that participation in this class is strictly voluntary and I freely chose to participate. I understand that Lovin' Soap Studio does not provide medical coverage for me. I verify that I will be responsible for any medical costs I incur as a result of my participation.

I understand that Sodium Hydroxide (Lye/NaOH) is a hazardous material and has the potential to create a highly reactive chemical reaction and that it may be dangerous or harmful if misused. _____ (Initial)

I understand that I am using this chemical at my own risk. While using this chemical I may encounter unavoidable risks or hazards where injuries may occur. I agree to release, hold harmless and indemnify Amanda Griffin, the owner of Lovin' Soap Studio and employees and agents, and any other people officially connected with this event from any liability for injury or damage that may occur in connection with my use of this chemical. I intend this release and indemnification to be effective, regardless of the type of legal recovery theory that may be chosen. I will make no claim or legal action against Amanda Griffin, the owner of Lovin' Soap Studio and employees and agents, and any other people officially connected with this event arising out of my use or misuse of this chemical during class or on my own time thereafter. _____ (Initial)

_____   _____
Participant Printed Name   Signature / Date

Having a signed release from a student does not automatically protect you from legal proceedings should an accident or injury occur. But a release, combined with insurance and safe instructional environment and procedures will go a long way to help protect you and your business.

Safe Instructional Environment and Procedures

The environment and the procedures you use during class should be safe and well tailored to your craft. In soapmaking we use sodium hydroxide. I would never teach in a facility that didn't have a sink for emergency rinsing. This contributes to a safe instructional environment. As an absurd and exaggerated example, *you wouldn't hold an art welding class at a gas station.*

Nor would I teach without requiring the appropriate safety gear for students to wear when handling the sodium hydroxide, which contributes to safe instructional procedures.

Another contributing factor to an unsafe instructional environment and procedures would be if you have a class that is too big for you to handle. You need to keep your class size manageable to help reduce your liability.

Amanda Gail

Soapmakers trying out their soap for the first time in Uganda.

raw

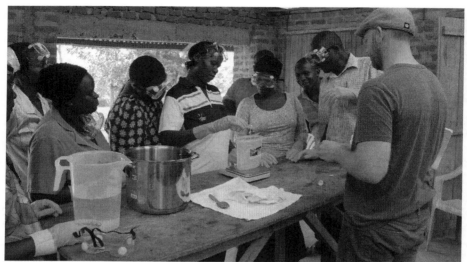
Amanda and Benjamin teaching soapmaking in Uganda.

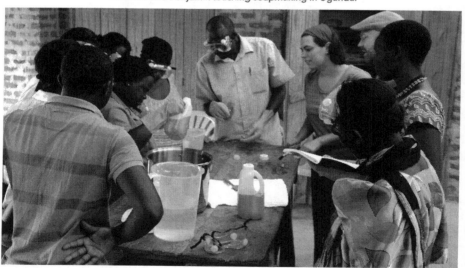

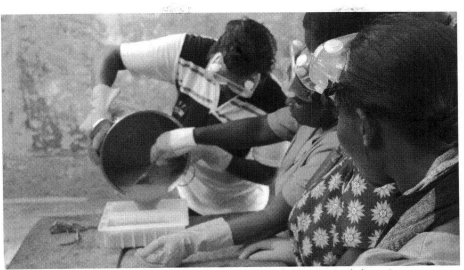

Project Lydia Soapmakers pouring soap in Uganda (www.projectlydia.org).

Teaching soapmaking in Uganda.

Chapter 13: Teaching in Developing Countries

Teaching in different countries with language barriers and in diverse economic situations is challenging and rewarding. This might be something you've never considered, but in case you have, this chapter is for you!

I've mentioned my not-for-profit, Lovin' Soap Project, an education-based organization that teaches soapmaking to women in underdeveloped or developing countries. With their learned comprehension of how soaps are formulated, what types of ingredients are necessary, and the instruction provided by the Lovin' Soap Project on local sourcing, women are empowered to make their own, inexpensive yet effective soaps to help maintain basic health and sanitation. Along with soapmaking, we teach business and marketing workshops to help women start a micro-business selling soap to earn money to support their families.

We are currently working in four countries; Haiti, Uganda, China and India. We teach soapmaking, but also business, marketing and goal setting workshops.

There is such a need for economic development in these types of countries and one great way to provide that is to teach trades. You might find that your craft or art is the perfect business opportunity for groups in developing communities. I've run across groups that create pottery, paper beads, painting, sewing and many other crafts. These items are sold in-country to tourists or exported to countries such as the United States, United Kingdom and France to be sold in boutique and specialty shops.

This won't be a complete how-to manual, but here are some general lessons learned and considerations when working in different countries to get you started.

As far as creating content and planning your workshops, the techniques in this book are a perfect starting point. We still provide hands-on workshops in which women get to make soap, just like my classes at home in the United States. Some things to consider:

The Culture

Whenever you travel to teach, you are a guest in a different culture. You should take the time to learn about the culture before you go and be respectful and considerate in regards to different religions, customs and daily life while visiting and conducting your workshops. For example, in Haiti, the women we teach embrace us with hugs and kisses and tons of affection in their greetings and goodbyes. The stark opposite is true with the women we teach in the Nakivumbi Village of Uganda. The major cultural mandate of the times for women is one of inferiority, thus not much affection is shown or given. To not take this into consideration would be ignorant and socially abrasive.

When planning workshop days, be sure to take note of special holidays and religious observances and avoid holding workshops on these days. If your workshop participants have other jobs, be sure to ask what days and times work best for them. In all the various groups we have taught, most of the women have children to look after, sometimes as many as 8 or 10, and they hustle to sell their foodstuffs and other provisions at local markets. They can't just quit their only source of income at the drop of a hat, so much planning and respect of time must be taken into consideration.

Sourcing Ingredients

When you teach your workshop in a different country, where will you purchase supplies? If you're lucky, you can perform a web search and find a supplier. Most of the countries that we work in don't have suppliers listed online. We've been lucky here and there, but sourcing ingredients usually involves driving around and walking through markets, asking any locals we can communicate with and often going on a wild goose chase.

You can always take materials, but we like to eventually support the local economy by purchasing materials in-country. We've been to bustling paper markets in Uganda to purchase magazine paper for paper-rolled beads and chaotic street markets in Haiti to find local oils and sodium hydroxide to use in soapmaking.

Always try to complete some sourcing ahead of time, as you don't want to get to the country and not be able to find materials. Hopefully, the contacts that you have in country can assist with sourcing.

Using Translators

All of the countries that we work in speak different languages. So when we teach workshops, we have to hire translators. A good translator can make or break your workshop and greatly influence the comprehension of your students depending on their skill as a translator. And always keep in mind the fine line between one who translates what you are saying to others and one who *interprets* what you are saying to others.

Support When You're Gone

This is a big one. Once you travel to a foreign country, teach the workshop and then go home, what happens to the group that you taught? If you taught them a trade to create a business, what sort of business training and support will they have? It's easy to learn a craft. The hard part is turning that knowledge into a business, which requires accounting, production, materials sourcing, wholesaling, payroll and everything else that goes along with running a business.

It is extremely expensive to travel to foreign countries and a follow-up trip might not be possible. If this is the case, partnering with an organization that works to provide economic development in communities might be the best option. There are many not-for-profits and organizations working in these countries that you can contact. With planning, they can provide the long-term support that these groups in developing countries need.

Amanda Gail

Chapter 14: Go Forth and Teach

If you've made it this far, you should now have an action plan to start your craft education business. Whether you are a painter, knitter, jewelry maker, soapmaker or cat hair weaver...you can earn a living or at least beef up your current income by teaching classes. I've included several pieces of advice that I deem important for this last section.

Be knowledgeable about your craft and current in techniques. You should know the ins and outs of what you are teaching. This might be a no-brainer but I want to emphasize this. I've seen teachers teaching outdated methods and approaches to their craft. Keep up to date with your craft's latest trends, supplies, and ingredients, whatever components make up your trade. If you have been doing your craft for twenty years, you might find that you are stuck in outdated methods or techniques.

Here's an example. My friend Holly learned to make soap from taking a class. In the class the students were instructed to stir their soap by hand and were not told that immersion blenders are standard these days and speed up the mixing process. Sometimes stirring by hand can take 20-30 minutes compared to 2-3 minutes using an immersion blender. This would have been a very useful thing to learn, whether or not the students hand-stirred the soap in class.

Keep your knowledge fresh and current. You can do this by reading new books, craft blogs, watching new technique videos on the Internet and attending conferences and seminars for your craft.

If you ever stop learning or honing your skills as a crafter, you will find that your classes can become irrelevant and outdated. Keep learning your craft! In doing so, your classes will always be current, fresh and up-to-date; which is what students are looking for.

As an instructor, don't be afraid to fail or afraid to own up to mistakes or lack of knowledge. Nobody is perfect and nobody knows absolutely every answer to every question. Don't act like you do. Your students will sniff out your fakeness from a mile away. Be genuine and honest.

For example, if a student asks a question in class that you cannot answer, answer honestly that you simply don't know. They will appreciate this and you will continually learn more about your craft. I have students that ask me questions about where ingredients come from or how they are made. I don't have the answer for every ingredient, as ingredients in soapmaking are expansive. I mention that I have no idea, but am excited to go home and look it up as I hope they do. If we have Internet and a few extra minutes, we can even look it up together in class.

Another example, if you are demonstrating a technique and it fails, don't sweat it. I've made soap before in advanced classes where the swirl didn't turn out perfectly or the cupcake topping wasn't piped quite right. It is the technique they are learning, not the final outcome. Sure it is not ideal, but everyone messes up every now and then. Make sure your instructions for the technique are solid and thorough. That's what counts.

So if you've been on the fence or you haven't really known where to start... just start! Start with your list of classes. Be bold. Be current. Go forth and teach!

About the Author

Amanda Gail has built her career around providing education in her craft, soapmaking. She has taught all over the United States in various classrooms and presents annually at conferences and seminars put on by the handcrafted soap industry's top guilds and organizations.

In 2008, after learning the craft of soapmaking, Amanda started an educational blog at LovinSoap.com, which features step-by-step full color photographic tutorials, articles, troubleshooting advice and general information about soapmaking. She publishes eZines (online magazines) and eBooks on the topic of soapmaking and has written for industry publications such as *Handmade Magazine, Saponifier and Soap Collaborative*.

In 2009, she started teaching classes in Dallas and Austin, providing hands-on workshops where students could totally immerse themselves in the craft of soapmaking and confidently learn the craft. Students from all over the United States have attended her hands-on workshops and even a few students have traveled from out of the country to attend!

In 2013 after a heart-moving trip to Haiti to teach a group of women who lived in a tent camp how to make soap, she decided that she would use her love of teaching to help as many women as possible in similar situations. With her partner, Benjamin Aaron, she created a not-for-profit whose aim was to teach women in developing nations the craft and the business of soapmaking, tackling two of poverty's biggest issues — lack of access to hygiene and lack of economic opportunity for women. The Lovin' Soap Project is a registered 501(c)(3) and is currently working in Haiti, Uganda, China and India and will continue to expand to other areas where women need opportunity.

Connect with Amanda online at www.teachcraftclasses.com and learn more about Lovin' Soap Project at www.lovinsoapproject.org!

Made in the USA
San Bernardino, CA
04 February 2019